WOUND UP

SO LIFE'S UNFAIR. And frustrating. And downright annoying at times. Maybe your parents haven't quite grasped the concept of independence and monitor every little thing you do — time spent on the computer, what you eat, homework, and your non-existent love life. Or worse yet, your mum tries to be "cool" and your dad busts a dance move in front of your new boyfriend. Sometimes even your friends do stupid stuff and drive you bonkers. Welcome to **LIFE 101.**

But don't go all gloomy on us just yet! There are **WAYS TO COPE** with life's little annoyances and major upsets. In *Wound Up*, you'll read stories from people just like yourself that can help you handle those irritating situations and figure out how you really feel. Try deciphering your mood with our

MOOD METER. Comfort yourself by cranking up your favourite tunes and dancing around with reckless abandon. Get it out, write it down, compose a song, punch a punchbag, create something and crumple it up. Don't be afraid to enlist a friend, go to your room or take a nice long walk. Find a place that makes you feel safe and secure — your personal **FRUSTRATION-FREE ZONE**. Things aren't always perfect.

Accept that and you just might be able to see things from a different (and less annoying) perspective. You may feel disappointed, misunderstood or alienated, but **NEVER UNDERESTIMATE** your ability to make your life — and maybe even the world — a much better place.

Table of Contents

Oh man!

like!

WOUND UP

PET WIND-UPS

" When people touch my hair.

Sneezing.

Biting nails.

Laziness.

Burping out loud.

🧑 *13*

Misspelt words!

Things that are out of place (e.g. a double light switch with each switch a different way).

People copying my words!

Weird smells.

Rude people!

🧑 *13* **"**

"Bare feet (toes).

People who eat with their mouth open.
🙍 18

I'm a neat freak. I hate mess or clutter.

Too much powder (the cover-up kind).

Pale, pasty skin. (Like mine! Minging!)
🙍 15"

PET WIND-UPS

"People who have major fashion faux pas.

I hate boys who think that they're a lot better than they actually are and always talk about themselves ("I'm so... ").

Monobrows — they make my tweezer finger itch!

Moustaches. I hate them. They look like dirt on a man's upper lip.

People who say "you know" after every single thing they say. YOU KNOW! Argh!

15 "

PET WIND-UPS

" Fake/superficial people.

Caked-on makeup.

Too-hard hugs.

Unnecessary swearing.

People putting themselves down.
🙍 17

Pastel colours.

My friends talking about a party they are going to that
I was not invited to in front of me.
🙍 12 "

66 Studying an area of a subject very diligently but having absolutely nothing about it included on the test. 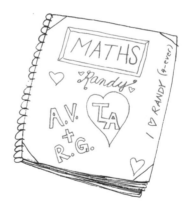 *12* **99**

PET WIND-UPS

"Fingernails on a blackboard.

When people use online talk in normal conversation (even if they're just joking).

Stereotypes.

Couples being all lovey-dovey around other people. I mean, if they kiss it's fine, but calling each other pet names… THAT'S obnoxious.

When people make fun of other people's disabilities (e.g. physical disabilities, learning problems, mental disorders like obsessive compulsive disorder and attention deficit disorder or things like dyslexia).

14 "

" Rap, hip-hop and pop music.

Boys' boxers showing above their jeans.

When people are mean to me.

When something shuts down on me — like the computer, or even a friend, when they just stop talking to mc all of a sudden.

13 **"**

POSERS

I hate people who pick on people younger than them.

I hate it when people think that they are tough, but they aren't.

I hate it when someone says "why?" all the time.
 15

Drivers with stereos on high in cars with open tops or windows.
 78 "

" My pet hate is a know-it-all that loves his/her own voice.

🧑 12

I hate people who don't mean what they say.

People who talk on their mobiles for no important reason.

People who are full of themselves.

I hate rule breakers.

People who are prejudiced.

🧑 19 **"**

LIFE WIND-UPS

"There are a lot of things in my life that piss me off. First is my ex-friend. Second is my family. Third is my school. It seems really small listed like that, but in truth it's not.

 14

The fact that nothing seems to be going right.

14 "

 Secondary school and stupid people.

 18

The way that my best friend's dad is so
innocent, yet he's dying of cancer.

13

" That I have so much homework.

14

Probably school. Also my mum —
she and I just can't agree on very much.

13 **"**

"Whenever I'm feeling pissed off, I would love it if people didn't state the obvious, like tell me, "You look like you're in a bad mood", or asking me if I'm okay. I'd rather they just leave me alone or make me laugh because sometimes laughter is the best medicine.

14

That I am sexually confused.

14"

"Society is really beginning to piss me off. Society, the media and peers mess up the lives of so many people. You are always reading about or hearing about ways to lose weight, what to eat, what to wear and the ideal woman/man. I think a lot of people focus too much on what others think. Why should it matter if you wear the latest style or what your weight is, as long as you are happy with the way you are?"

14

" OK, who isn't pissed off a lot? I know I am. The stuff that angers me the most and the fastest has to be the endless school gossip, quick judgements that people make along with nasty glares and most of all the lack of ability I have to get along with my parents. It just does NOT ever happen. *16* **"**

TEACHER WIND-UPS

The worst statements teachers have up their sleeves.

That's exercises 5 through 16 for tonight, not 5 and 16.

The paper upside down on your desk is an assessment. Get started now.

Your answer is correct, but not to that question.

_____(insert your name here), see me after class.

If that note you're reading is so interesting, I think I'll read it aloud so the rest of the class can enjoy it as well.

We'll make up the time you've just wasted in here after school.

I'm considering recommending you for summer school.

I'm sure your parents are going to enjoy hearing about this behaviour.

FAMILY WIND-UPS

" My mum! Sometimes she's really sweet, but most of the time she's screaming at me, mostly for things she's done! If she misplaces her keys or something, it's somehow my fault! I hate her! I can't wait to get out of the house so I don't have to listen to her say how stupid and worthless I am.

🧑 15

My sister can be extremely cute and nice, but at the same time she can be a pain. She has Down Syndrome. She doesn't always listen to people and her favourite word to say is "no".

🧑 13 "

" My parents are total hypocrites. My dad thinks he's God and my mum is just out there.

15

I hate it when parents do stuff, and then say you can't do it because you're a kid.

12

I hate it when my parents worry too much about something so small. And I hate it when my parents look at the negative side of what I'm telling them.

19 "

33

❝A lot of things are going wrong right now. My relationship with my dad is very on again /off again. Sometimes I feel like I have to be the adult because he acts like a baby. It's really hard for me because I'm not a person to go and tell everyone what's going on in my life. I keep most things inside, and I don't know if that's a good or bad thing. It's hard to keep everything in. 16 ❞

RIEND WIND-UPS

"I'm so amazingly jealous of my best friend. Somehow, everything he does is better than what I can do. Everything he does is amazing and great, while my accomplishments are mediocre and meaningless.

 15

Nothing really annoys me about my best friend. We all have our faults and none of hers really bother me.

15 14

Friends who call me gay at inappropriate times.

14 "

The one thing I would change about my friend is to have her not be so hard on me. She does it because she wants to help, but she's always like, "Is your maths homework done yet?" and if I say no, she'll be like, "Well, why not? It should be finished by now. Why didn't you finish it last night?" She acts like my mum!!

15

"My best friend is a REAL scatterbrain! We share a locker and it's always full of her stuff. And she breaks anything I have in there. She doesn't do her work — she just sits back and copies mine and flirts with this muppet who uses girls (and all of her friends have told her how bad and stupid he is). She's really nice but she can be REALLY annoying sometimes!"

13

BITE YOUR TONGUE

WORDS THAT ANNOY

"Dude". And just swearing.
18

When people pronounce "nuclear" as "nucular".
Hate it. It is clearly spelt with nothing separating
the "c" and the "l". It's not so hard to read. It
particularly bugs me when it's mispronounced
as such by certain leaders of certain powerful
countries — ahem. One who has the power to
use "weapons of mass destruction" should have
the capacity to pronounce them.
15

There are a few words/phrases that I say that get on
my nerves. They include: "oh man", "whatever",
"retard", "ugly" and "stupid".
14

ya know

like!

❝ I've tried not to say the word "like" for an entire day, just for the heck of it... but that failed. 14

One word I say that really annoys me is "like". Sometimes I can't help saying it, though. 12 **❞**

ugly!

Oh man!

SONGS THAT ANNOY

" "Hey Mickey You're So Fine".
 18

A song that drives me insane is "It's A Small World".
18 17

Anything by Britney Spears, *NSYNC, Backstreet
Boys, etc.
15 "

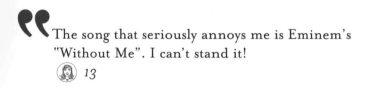 The song that seriously annoys me is Eminem's "Without Me". I can't stand it!

 13

Rap and R&B songs about bitches and money.

 17

EXPRESSIONS THAT ANNOY

" I say "Lordith". My friend made it up, but I say it every two words. It's so annoying after a while.
🙍 13

MY expressions that people copy! Also, "Say what?"
🙍 13 "

ANNOYING ANSWERS

The worst answering machine messages

1. A long rambling outgoing message essentially saying 'leave a message".

2. Loud music with no message.

3. A very long pause between the message and the beep.

4. Multiple beep beep beep beep beeps.

5. "Hi I'm not home, but you already know that".

6. "I'm either on the computer or picking my nose or cutting off a hangnail that's been driving me crazy all day..."

7. Little kid blabbering, "weave a wessage".

8. Operator coming on with, "the party you are trying to reach is not home, would you like to pay £5 to leave a message with our special service?"

MOODY JUDY

MOOD METER

Reading Your Mood

1. Take a moment (and a deep breath) and check in with yourself. What does your gut say?

2. Notice how you're reacting to what (and who) is around you. (Are you snapping back at your boyfriend? Tuning out your little sis? Going all soft during a toothpaste advert?)

3. Check your body for signs (i.e. tense shoulders, clenched fists, crinkled brow etc.).

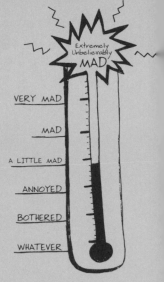

4. Watch your walk. (Are your strides long and slow, or short and quick? Are you dragging your feet, or do you have a little spring in your step?)

5. And if you're still clueless, buy a mood ring!

MOOD READER

Reading Others' Moods

1. Listen. Instead of planning a response, be really quiet and simply listen to what is being said. You can learn a lot by paying attention.

2. Pay attention to facial expressions. Is the person smiling or looking sad? Is their forehead scrunching up or are they on the verge of tears?

3. Watch the person in action. Is he/she throwing things, or acting aggressively? Is your friend stroppier than usual?

4. Take note of any major behaviour changes. Is your friend eating less or talking about feeling worthless? Shopping excessively or binge-drinking? Extreme behaviour can be a cry for help.

5. If all else fails, and your intuitive self can't get a clear reading, ask! Sometimes a heartfelt conversation from a concerned friend can make all the difference!

DEEP DARK DAYS

"I was seriously depressed during Years 9 and 10. I'd had bulimia for a year and had been struggling with my weight since Year 8. My body issues were stupid. I'm not fat now and I wasn't back then, but a boy didn't like me so I decided it was me. I ate carrots — only carrots — for a whole week. Then crackers. But I found I couldn't do without food so I ate and decided to throw it up. When I finally got help, it got worse. I had serious self-confidence issues and the friends I was going round with were not very nice. My school life was miserable, but I always went back the next day with a smile on my face. I became someone different than I actually was. One day, my best friend said to me, "What happened to you? What happened to the person I met a year ago?" I couldn't answer him. So I decided to work on it. I started doing things I wanted to do, not caring what others thought and I slowly became happy again.

15"

" I have thought about suicide. I think about all the people who would come to my funeral and cry, and that makes me realise how many friends I really have and how many people wouldn't be the same without me doing stupid stuff just to make them laugh.

 13 **"**

"I've thought about suicide, but there are so many ways to kill yourself that by the time I've decided how to kill myself, I've talked myself out of it. Like this morning, I was sitting on my roof deciding if I should jump or if it would hurt less to get run over by a truck when I saw the school bus stop for my two little sisters. As they crossed the street, hand in hand, I realised that I loved them too much and would disappoint them if I hurt myself. I taught them to hold hands and look both ways before crossing the street. But at the same time, I was thinking I don't deserve them — they are perfect little angels. And before I knew what I was doing, I was climbing down into my room and pulling on my jacket to go to school.

13"

CREATURE
COMFORTS

CHICKEN SOUP & OTHER COMFORTING TRICKS

" When I'm down and blue, what makes me feel
better (after punching my pillow), is listening to
music. Every type. Rap when it's a bad situation,
angry music like Linkin' Park when I'm 110%
pissed off, or Dave Matthews when I need
comforting. Other activities that aid me in
expressing my anger are working out (gets all
that adrenaline going) or going on a sun bed
(even though it's extremely bad for you).
16

Turning up my music really
loud and dancing around.
18 "

My dog comforts me. You can't be sad around her; she just automatically makes you happy.

13

Ice cream, my boyfriend or some Blink 182.

14

When I am feeling sad or depressed, I like to do something where I can completely forget about everything bad that happened. Things like watching TV, going on the computer, reading and sleeping.

13

" Music. And that's it.
🙂 14

Writing in my diary and writing songs.
🙂 13

When I am down I love to eat ice cream, get comfy on the couch and turn on a good video while holding my guinea pig.
🙂 13

I sit alone in my room and do something I feel like, usually listening to my favourite music groups (ABBA works best) or I draw or watch my fave TV shows.
🙂 13 **"**

"Chocolate and music are pretty much my solution for any problem.
15

When I'm feeling down, my cat usually comforts me. She makes me feel good about myself because she can't tell me how to act or that I'm being too dramatic. She just sits there and in a strange way listens to me. Every time I see her, I smile and feel good about myself, even if she is just sitting there not paying any attention to me. I know she always cares.
13 "

COMFORT FROM A FRIEND

❝What's comforting is the thought of my friends and their comments about how boring life would be without me and how much talent I have.

🧑 13

Comfort and support. That's the best anyone could do. Or give me something to break. My friend gave me a cup and hammer once. That was fun.

🧑 14

Give me a hug, tell me things will be OK and make me laugh.

🧑 14 ❞

"People being nice to me and caring. It's always nice to know that someone cares about me.

 13

When I am really mad, I like my friends to say sympathetic things that make me feel like I can make it through this and my life will go on. I am very lucky; I have many wonderful friends that are all very caring. They support and comfort me whenever I am mad or sad.

 13

I just want them to go away so I can cool off. You can't cool off with friends there — they just make it worse.

 13 "

MAJORLY
WOUND-UP
MOMENTS

MOST ANGRY

"I act like Godzilla with PMS.
 *15*

I become distant and do poorly in school.
15 **"**

❞ I remember being really angry with my best friend who was really clever and a talented artist because the school heartthrob took an interest in her. He was a year above us and suddenly nothing mattered but him and his cliquey friends. I felt betrayed, left out and angry.

P.S. They got married when we left school, she never went to college and he went into his father's construction company. One time when I was visiting after college one of her best friends told me that she had an affair with the groom-to-be just before they got married. I never told my friend about it and still see them occasionally, 30 years later. They have three kids and one grandchild. I always felt angry towards her mother because she was the one that said being a wife and mum was what you do. Thinking you need to be married for happiness really winds me up. Although I'm happily married, I still feel as though women need to be taught independence.

 51 ❞

MOST FRUSTRATED

"Whenever I'm in maths
and I just don't get it.
14"

PISSED OFF POETICS

1775 "Pesky", meaning "annoying" from the word "pesty", meaning a pest plagues.

1811 "MIFF", MEANING "ANNOY".

1836 "RILE", MEANING "INFURIATES".

1908 "PEEVE" OR "PEEVED", MEANING "TO ANNOY".

1949 "BUG", MEANING "ANNOYING".

1910 "Get Someone's Goat"; Buster Keaton first used it, meaning "to agitate".

1925 "Hit the Roof", meaning "really annoyed". Also, 1928 "Blow ones top", and 1938 "Blow a fuse".

1931 "Burn Up" Sinclair Lewis used "What burns me up" to mean "makes me really mad".

1955 "Teed Off", meaning "angry".

1970's "to Piss Off", used by Rolling Stone magazine meaning "to make someone really mad".

1971 "Snit", meaning "fit of rage".

69

MOST UNFAIR

"One of my friends was being picked on for being white and when I stood up for him, I was told I was too weak to fight because I was white. So I hit him right in his jaw!

 15"

MOST UPSET

"Watching my aunt when she was in hospital and seeing her eyes move while she could see us sobbing for her, but she still couldn't move. And then going to her funeral.
14

When I disappointed my grandma after she took me on a trip to Costa Rica.
15

When my parents got divorced.
14"

 When three of my best friends thought I had told my boyfriend their biggest secret, but I hadn't. I felt like crap and they had no right to accuse me of that. They wouldn't listen and were being really mean to me – silent treatment (so stupid).

14

"When I was told that a boy I liked didn't like me. That always hurts. Rejection can't be good, ever. But you can only learn from it.

 14

When I knew I couldn't get back together with the love of my life.

 14 "

" When my dad hit me on the head and on the arm. It hurt like hell. I had been yelling at him and he had been yelling at me for a while, and then he got really angry and hit me. I was so stunned that I stopped mid-sentence and fled to my room. I cried for hours. I couldn't stop. That was the first time my dad had hit me since I was three. Even a nice hot shower couldn't cool me down – I went on bawling. I pretended to be sick the next day and curled up into a little ball under my covers in the downstairs shower cos that's where I go when I feel bad. I was down for days. I finally got better, but the relationship between my dad and me was changed forever. I don't even know why he hit me. I never have forgiven him for that – and never will.

🎀 13 **"**

MOST MISUNDERSTOOD

"I'm ALWAYS misunderstood. Everyone thinks I'm this weak little girl, but I can kick the crap out of boys as good as the next girl. I'm sick of being thought of as innocent and harmless.

15

The hardest thing about being a teenager is feeling so misunderstood. I try to explain how I feel and my friends and family always misinterpret me. Also it's hard being vertically challenged and constantly being made fun of. People don't realise how much it hurts to be made fun of until they are the victims.

14

Always. I'm very unique and introverted, so I am often misunderstood.

14 "

STINGS LIKE
A BEE

BEHIND-YOUR-BACK CHATTER

" In Year 7, everyone hated me. I don't even remember why now. It was probably about a friendship dispute or something. I even hated myself. I came home every night crying. Everyone was pissed off at me and I ate my lunch alone in a corner and waited for some kids to come up and say they hated me. That's when I started to try drugs. It was beautiful and horrible at the same time. When my friends started to accept me again because I said I was sorry for whatever I did for the thousandth time, I stopped doing drugs. It was really hard to stop, but I did it. I made a promise to myself never again to even try drugs again. Please don't tell my parents, they don't know and I don't want them to. Ever.

13 "

"This girl told my deepest secret to everyone.
I didn't talk to her for three months.

 15"

SHOULD HAVE WIRED IT SHUT

" Whenever my friends tell me things, I always keep my mouth shut unless they say otherwise. My best friend had been going out with this girl for about seven months. They were very serious. He had told me about this time when he was in Mexico and had got together with this other girl. I kept it secret for a long time, but then one day it slipped out and I ended up telling his girlfriend everything. She seemed to take it well, but then that night she called me and she was really upset. She didn't know if she should break up with him or not. Then my friend called me and was crying as well. He wasn't pissed off at me at all. They had a hard time working it out, and I was in the middle. They ended up staying together and now they probably love each other more than they did before. But I probably should have kept my mouth shut.

16 "

I never keep my mouth shut if I have something to say. People should hear it, although sometimes I regret what I say. 15

DROPPED FOR A BOY

"In the middle of my cousin's bar mitzvah, this blonde-haired girl came in. She is one of those girls who can get any boy she wants, whenever she wants him. The minute she set foot in that party, all the boys stuck to her like glue. Of course, the boy that I liked was attracted to her. She flirted with him, and he flirted back. She knew very well that I liked him and that he liked me, but she went ahead and hugged him and flirted with him in front of my face. When I saw her, I wanted to burst out crying in my mum's arms. I felt betrayed and my heart was broken. Even though he lived far away, I still had feelings for him. I questioned myself as to why he liked her instead of me. Was she that much better than me? I was so upset. When I left, I saw him on the dance floor holding her. The other girl had bigger boobs and was taller than me. But these are things I cannot help. Shouldn't boys be mature enough to look past that?

14"

PARENTAL WIND-UPS

ANNOYING HABITS

"My mother is a great person, but she drives me insane. It's as if she needs to repeat herself a million times just to get one semi-conscious thought out of her head. It is annoying because I know she is an intelligent person, but most of the time I feel like I can never communicate with her.

 19

My mum picks her nose in the car. It's disgusting. But I still love and accept her anyway.

15"

"My dad does not really annoy me, but I hate it when my mum patronises me and my friends right in front of me.

 15

They talk soooo much.

 14 "

I hate it how my mum's always in control. My dad can't make one decision without her knowing, yet she seems to do quite well without his input. Imagine what my weekends are like when she leaves the house to go shopping for a whole day! "Dad, can I go out shopping?" "Dunno... call Mum." And of course her mobile is never on... so my weekends are spent at home wishing that my dad could actually make one decision by himself.

15

EMBARRASSING

" Mum gets drunk and passes out with her mouth open in front of friends. Dad is mean to my friends, a total arsehole.

 14

My mum had the DJ at a party announce that she was there to pick me up.

 14 "

" My dad dances. It doesn't matter where he dances, it's just the fact that he dances. It is just soooooooo embarrassing.

 13 **"**

UNFAIR RULES

MUM'S RULES
1. No Black.
2. Hair-tied back and neat.
3. No "grown-up" movies.
4. No shopping without mum.
5. Always listen to mum !!!

"Now, I am allowed to do pretty much whatever I want… within reason. But until I was 12 my mum was a stickler. Here are some rules I had: I wasn't allowed to wear black, wasn't allowed to wear my hair down and wasn't allowed to see 12 films (till I was actually 12!). But when I was 13, I was allowed to do more than most of my friends including: going to the cinema without adults, wearing heavy makeup and going shopping unsupervised.

15 "

" My parents monitor every little thing I do, everything I eat, how much time I spend on the computer, if I've done my homework, etc. I'm the youngest of four but I'm old enough to take care of my own life! I'm aware of the time and I know how much homework I have and how much time it'll take to do, but my mum just says I'm "giving her cheek" when I try to explain that to her!

 13 **"**

FRUSTRATING

"My mum tries to solve the world's problems. She's a therapist for a living and so she has lots of practise with other people's problems. So when it comes to home and family, Mum leaves and the therapist comes in. It's awful.

 13

When parents act like they're cool.

 14 "

"I hate it when my mum interrupts to tell me not to interrupt her, says we always have to have the last word when she really does, and when my dad does stuff we can't do and says it's because he's 43.

13

It seems like my parents favour my brother. They always buy him clothes and let him go out whenever. When he comes in late he never seems to get in trouble. It's really annoying.

14 "

My mum tries to give me advice on stuff she has no clue about, like football and horseback riding.

15

"They don't realise that nothing really changes in five minutes and if it does I will call them. I feel like I have to tell them every time I take a step or scratch my head. God forbid they let me stay out an extra hour. If they really think about it, it's another hour that they get to stay home, warm and cosy. The other thing that really gets me is that they never let me explain. I know the difference between an excuse and an explanation, and I just want to explain things sometimes. Maybe when they hear my side of the story they will realise what kind of pressure I was under or why I thought what I did was OK or whatever the situation may be.

 16 "

QUEEN/KING
FOR A DAY

WHAT I'D CHANGE ABOUT THE WORLD

"If I was queen for a day, I would stop war, ban all bad music and bad people, make everything coloured prettily, and take maths off the planet.
12

WORLD PEACE!! War is beyond nightmare.
15 "

WHAT I'D CHANGE ABOUT MY LIFE

"I would make it so that I could leave the world whenever I felt like it.

🧑 14

I would add two more hours to my day so I could do more.

🧑 17 "

WHAT I'D CHANGE ABOUT MY PARENTS

" I'd make my mum signal when she changed lanes and press the clear button when she's finished using the microwave.

16

I would change my parents so that they would know when I don't want them around, or not to bug me so don't have to get mad at them.

13 "

I would make my parents less uptight and turn them back into their true hippie selves that they used to be. There's a little hippie in all of them trying to get out. 15

Make Love Not War

WHAT I'D CHANGE
ABOUT MY FRIENDS

" Get Dylan to be nicer, Erin to shut up
and listen, and Lauren to not be so rude
to people.
13

Make my friend less snobby and self-centred.
15 "

WHAT I'D CHANGE ABOUT MYSELF

"I tend to run away from situations I don't like. I wish I had enough guts to take in what's happening. There are some things in life that you can only learn from experiencing them. If I run away from things then I'll be missing a lot. I think it's important to be able to talk about things. I would change that about me.

 16 "

"If I could change one thing about myself, it would be to have more self-confidence and (at an earlier age) not be so concerned what others think about me. I think I got derailed at a couple of points in my life (drugs, dropping the people who were really good friends, losing sight of my dreams) by not believing in myself enough — and by being willing to compromise what I really believed so that the people I thought were cool (then) would want to have me around. I got lucky — I was never arrested and I realised in time that I didn't like the direction I was heading. I cleaned up my act, got the school to let me go back and got a degree… but there are friendships that never recovered and I regret that.

 45 "

IF I WERE IN CHARGE...

You could decide what time you had to be in, and tell your parents when to be home.

Toilet seats would automatically go back down.

You could absorb all the maths equations and history dates while playing sports and watching TV.

Leaves would rake themselves and weeds would pull themselves.

Homework would be limited to half an hour.

You could drive when you were ten — and there would be no accidents, ever.

There would be a robot that cleaned your room and did ALL the dishes.

School would only be at the weekend — and every other day would be holiday.

Stress could be turned into petrol and used to run cars.

BLOWING
OFF STEAM

FAIL-SAFE STRESS RELEASE

"Usually I turn on my favourite radio station or lose myself in my headphones. It depends on my mood. Music really has an influence on how I'm feeling, so if I need to lift myself from the stress I play some upbeat music. If that doesn't work, I know that I can always count on my friends.

🙎 13 "

" I tend to swear a lot and that gets me in trouble, the I get more pissed off.
18

When I'm pissed off I shut people out for just a little while because I'm afraid that if I have a conversation with them they'll think I'm being rude.
13

I tend to lose my temper, but music always helps.
14 **"**

" Spilling everything in
a letter to myself, or
talking to and seeing my boyfriend.
🧑 14

I tend to ignore my friends. Then I usually direct
my anger at some unsuspecting victim, and apologise
soon afterwards. My rage is a tickling feeling on the
top of my knuckles that will only be appeased when
contacted with human flesh. I don't allow my
knuckles to be appeased. Testosterone is the
bane of my existence.
🧑 16 "

"I usually hold it in and it feels like HELL. Sometimes I let it out when I'm alone. I lie on my bed and just cry.

13

I have a sort of hard time releasing stress. I just bury it away and try to avoid dealing with it. When I do release it, it is usually in the form of artwork, baking or loud music.

15

When I get really pissed off (or sad), I usually try not to show it. Then, I use that energy playing football. But otherwise, I go to my room or just chill out with good friends of mine so I can forget about whatever happened.

15

I either blow up or start to clean.

14 "

FAVOURITE HIDE-OUTS

"When I'm really pissed off or sad, I like to be outside. I just have to get away from everything. I go to the quietest, most natural place I can find. If I am not allowed to leave the house, I just sink into the darkest corner I can find. Otherwise, I go to a park or something. I just need to be outdoors and away from people. It calms me down a lot and lets me think.

👧 15"

"I use my punch bag and turn on angry music or light candles and take a bath." 14

TUNES TO TAKE THE EDGE OFF

"I'm OK" – Christina Aguilera

"Complicated" – Avril Lavigne

"Teenage Angst" – Placebo

"Jagged Little Pill" – Alanis Morissette

"Dammit" – Blink 182

"Longview" – Green Day

"Stop" – Jane's Addiction

"We're Not Gonna Take It" – Twisted Sister

"Cool Thing" – Sonic Youth

"Everybody Hurts" – REM

"I Love To Hate You" – Erasure

"Hold On" – Sarah McLachlan

"Drops Of Jupiter" – Train

"Blue Monday" – New Order

"Somebody" – Depeche Mode

"I like to go to the downstairs shower. I don't turn it on – I just sit there and think about things and what's going on and how to deal with it. It just makes the whole world shut up and listen to me, if only for a minute or two.
13

When I am pissed off, I go to my room or go for a walk. In my room, I feel safe and secure, so that's where I usually go.
16"

"I go to my room to sort out my thoughts. Sometimes I sit there feeling sorry for myself for long periods of time. Other times, I go somewhere with a person I trust to take my mind off things.

 13

The bathroom at home or school – it's private. At school we call it 'bathroom time'!

15

It's always best to change your room into a comfortable place if it isn't already. I burn incense, listen to music and talk on the phone. I also write in my diary.

15"

" I usually go for a drive. It helps me unwind and sometimes I just really enjoy being alone on a windy country road.
 19 **"**

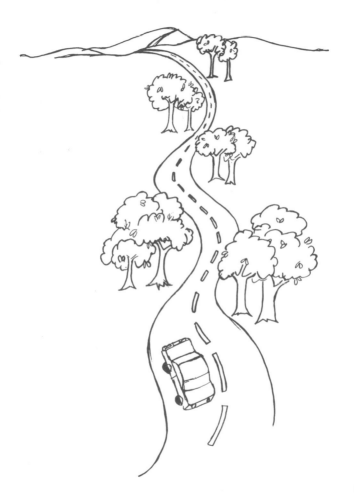

FANTASY PUNISHMENTS

Fantasy Penalties for Pet Wind-Ups

The Story Repeater: Tongue lopped off and fed to stray dogs.

The Braggart: All mates laugh and point each time he/she walks into the room. No explanation given — ever.

The Interrupter: Bird poos on head each time he/she cuts anyone off mid-sentence (even when indoors).

The Whiner: Frog literally gets stuck in throat.

The Chronically Late: Sleeps through final exams and has to repeat entire year.

The Neglectful Borrower: New trousers tear each time he/she bends over until 21st birthday.

The Kiss Up: Permanently loses ability to blink. Teeth fall out.

The Fair-Weather Friend: Is stricken with chronic bad breath and sweaty palms.

The Social Climber: Forced to take job handing out fliers on busy street corner dressed as a chicken.

The Table Tapper: Loses thumbs in freak boating accident. Hair grows on palms.

FANTASY PUNISHMENTS VISUALISED

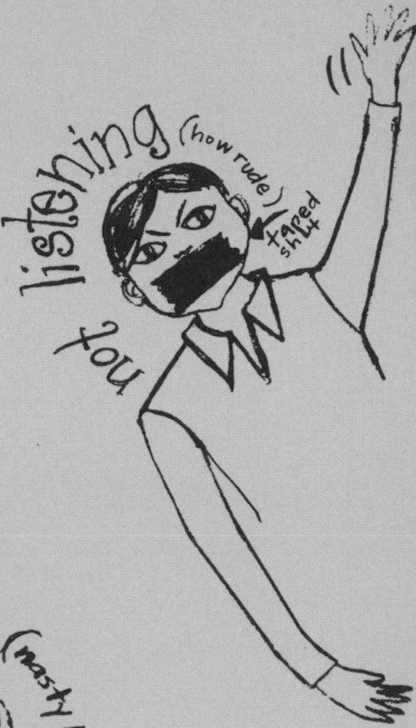

Thank you to all the teen contributors.
(This is a listing of those who wished to be named.)

Jessica Adnett

Iris Brilliant

Jordan Bamberger

Madeliene Barab

Becca Bartels

Surya Bhat

Christian Boe

Hannah Byers-Straus

Emily Cafaro

John Cafaro

Cat Callaway

Caty Cote

Courtney Czerwinski

Emily Dindial

Eric Durbrow

Daphne Earp

Elektra Fike-Data

Rachel Freier-Miller

Becky Fresch

Brent Gabel

Roxanne Garrity

Katie Greer

Brittany Guianen

Omid Hashemi

Sierra Hixon

Abby Huston

Micaela Irvin

Neima Jahromi

Zoe Janachek

Abby Kernan-Schloss

Ariel Krietzman

Venyce Larry

Darin Martin

Brendan McEnter

Kim Moyer

Ayanna
  Murry-Mazini

Caitlyn Nally

Veronica Pellitteri

Allison Proba

Annie Ramoso

Adam Rice

Liz Mutter-
  Rottmeyer

Hayley Roy

Evan Schaffer

Cameron Shafer

Emiko Shimabukuro

Ellyn Sidell

Marcy Silver

Sarah Thabault

Alex Vaenberg

Alex von Eckartsberg

Anusheh Warda

Lindy Waterman

Annabelle Watts

Casey Withrow